Investment Appraisal:

A Simple Introduction

Also by K.H. Erickson

Simple Introductions

Choice Theory
Financial Economics
Game Theory
Game Theory for Business
Investment Appraisal
Microeconomics

Investment

Appraisal:

A Simple Introduction

K.H. Erickson

© 2013 K.H. Erickson

All rights reserved.

No part of this publication may be reproduced, stored in or introduced into a retrieval system, or transmitted in any form or by any means, including electronic, mechanical, photocopying, recording or otherwise, without the prior permission of the author.

Contents

1 Introduction   6
2 Accounting Rate of Return (ARR)   9
2.1 ARR and ROCE Explained   9
2.2 ARR Extended Examples   13
2.3 Problems with ARR   26
3 Payback Period (PP)   31
3.1 Payback Period Explained   31
3.2 Payback Period Extended Examples   36
3.3 Problems with Payback Period   44
4 Net Present Value (NPV)   49
4.1 NPV Explained   49
4.2 NPV Using Discount Tables and Excel   59
4.3 NPV Extended Examples   64
5 Internal Rate of Return (IRR)   71
5.1 IRR Explained   71
5.2 IRR Extended Examples, IRR in Excel   74
5.3 Problems with IRR   81
6 Investment Appraisal in Practice   84
6.1 Potential Sources of Error   84
6.2 Risk Management   88
6.3 Project Management   96

1 Introduction

In order to survive and grow businesses must make decisions involving investments in new buildings, vehicles, machinery, equipment, shares, or other long-term assets. The central feature of these decisions is time, and an investment involves incurring financial costs at one point in time to gain greater benefits at another, usually later, point in time. This outlay also typically comes as one large investment, while the benefits will usually arrive in smaller amounts over an extended period.

Making the correct investment decisions is crucial to a business for two main reasons. First, the investments will often involve significant amounts of resources, and a business may make an expenditure representing a large proportion of their total wealth and assets. If the decision is made poorly then it could have damaging or even devastating effects on the future of the business. Second, it may be impossible or very expensive to abandon an investment project once it has begun. An investment made by a business will typically be tailored to its own unique needs, and this specialization is likely to limit the value it holds to other possible users who will naturally have different needs, and in turn reduce the money that could be recouped from the investment.

Investment decisions are of vital importance to the viability of a business, and as a result it's essential that all investment proposals are properly screened before they proceed. A crucial part of this screening process is the use of appropriate methods of evaluation and appraisal. In practice there are four basic methods used by businesses worldwide to evaluate investment opportunities, noting that ARR and ROCE follow the same approach:

1) Accounting rate of return (ARR) / return on capital employed (ROCE);

2) Payback period (PP);

3) Net present value (NPV);

4) Internal rate of return (IRR).

Some businesses may use a variation of these four methods, and others may not use any investment appraisal method at all, ignoring facts and figures to instead make decisions based on emotions and what feels right. But in practice most businesses around the world appear to use one of the four methods listed above.

The next four chapters explain and assess each of the appraisal methods in turn, using a range of numerical examples to show how the method is calculated, and investigate the strengths and weaknesses associated with each measure while making comparisons between them. Simple steps to calculate the NPV and IRR of projects using Excel are also given, to facilitate quicker and easier investment appraisal. The final chapter looks at how project appraisal is conducted in practice, and the additional issues that a business may need to manage.

2 Accounting Rate of Return (ARR)

2.1 ARR and ROCE Explained

The accounting rate of return (ARR) takes the average annual accounting profit that an investment is expected to generate, before expressing it as a percentage of the average investment made in the project to earn that profit, measured in accounting terms:

ARR = (Average annual profit / Average investment) x 100%

For example, it may already be known that the average annual profit for a project is £20,000 and its average investment is £80,000.

$$ARR = (£20,000 / £80,000) \times 100\%$$
$$= 0.25 \times 100\%$$
$$= 25\%$$

Alternatively, the information may not be so easily presented, and some additional calculations may have to be made. Perhaps a business invests £50,000 at the start of an investment project, and another £40,000 after one year, making a total of two investments. In return it expects to achieve an income stream of £110,000 each year over the next five years, starting from the time of the initial investment.

$$\text{Average annual investment profit} = £110,000 / 5$$
$$= £22,000$$

$$\text{Average investment} = (£50,000 + £40,000) / 2$$
$$= £90,000 / 2$$
$$= £45,000$$

$$ARR = (£22,000 / £45,000) \times 100\%$$
$$= 0.4889 \times 100\%$$
$$= 48.89\%$$

These calculations are quite simple, and the formula and examples here give the general idea of what the accounting rate of return is all about.

ARR and the return on capital employed (ROCE) ratio follow the same approach with investment appraisal, and both relate the accounting profit to the costs of the investment used to generate this profit. The difference is that ROCE is a popular method to assess the performance of business investments after they are finished, while ARR assesses a particular investment's potential performance before it has began.

The use of ARR would involve the setting of a minimum target ARR that an investment must meet. This minimum target may be based on the rate that previous investments made by the business had actually achieved, measured by the post-investment ROCE, and as a business wouldn't want to accept lower rates than they knew were achievable this may be a good starting point. Alternatively, the minimum target could be the industry-average ROCE, as a business ultimately needs to keep up with its competitors if it is to survive. If a number of different investment proposals under consideration all appeared likely to exceed this minimum rate of return, then the project with the highest ARR would usually win out.

Any privately owned business is typically aiming to increase the wealth levels of its owner, and as a result ARR may seem an appealing method to evaluate investment opportunities. The profit included in the ARR calculation can be seen as a net wealth rise over a period, and relating it to the level of investment responsible can be seen as accounting for the associated cost, giving an overall approach that seems logical and intuitive.

ARR is thought to have several advantages as an investment appraisal method. The ROCE, which can be thought of as a post-investment ARR, is widely used as a business performance measure, and a firm's shareholders are believed to use the financial ratio to evaluate the performance of management, while the financial goals of a business may also be expressed using a target ROCE. With this in mind it may seem correct to use an investment appraisal method which is consistent with general business performance evaluation. The fact that ARR or ROCE are given as a percentage may also be a significant factor in their use, as managers may feel more comfortable using measures expressed in percentage terms that they can easily understand.

The next section will include more detailed examples, including some additional factors that an investment project may involve in reality, to see how ARR copes with these issues in practice.

2.2 ARR Extended Examples

The four examples here will be repeated for all four investment appraisal techniques; ARR; Payback Period; NPV; and IRR. This will give the complete picture of the predicted investment performance, and allow a direct comparison between the four methods to potentially reveal what is lacking in each in practice.

As a simplifying assumption it will be assumed that the cash flows in and out are paid or received at the end of each yearly period. In reality this wouldn't be the case, as employees would need to be paid on a far more frequent basis, and it's also highly unlikely that any business would accept waiting until the end of the year to be paid for a service it has delivered. But this assumption shouldn't change the analysis to any significant extent and it's often made in the real life use of accounting and finance, to remove the uncertainty caused by unpredictable payment schedules. For example, this method allows December's sales to always be assigned to one year, and the following January's sales to the next. This removes the situation where a firm may appear to have suffered a downturn in fortunes over a certain year, when in reality it's simply a case of December's sales being paid straight away one year, and not being paid until the following January in the year of the apparent downturn.

One issue that's likely to be a common factor in investments but has not been considered so far is the problem of depreciation. This is the decline in value that will naturally occur in an invested asset over time, due to either expected wear and tear, or a general reduction in market value as newer products replace it. The following example includes depreciation costs in its analysis.

Example 1: Cooper & Stone

Cooper & Stone, a manufacturing business, is considering a significant investment in an advanced machine to improve its scope, and enable the introduction of a potentially lucrative business service. The provision of the service would depend upon an investment of £100,000 for the machine, which must be paid immediately. Once the machine is up and running it's expected to create service sales for the next five years, which are thought to grow steadily at first as the new service business segment gains popularity with customers. Then growth is expected to stagnate as sales stay at a constant level, before sales fall rapidly as the machine nears the end of its life and becomes less efficient and productive. At the end of the five year period the machine is estimated to have a resale value of £25,000.

Sales of the service are expected to proceed as follows:

Next year = 10,000 units sold;
Two years ahead = 15,000 units sold;
Three years ahead = 20,000 units sold;
Four years ahead = 20,000 units sold;
Five years ahead = 5,000 units sold.

Estimations suggest that the new service product can be sold at a price of £10 per unit, and that the variable costs for the new business service will come to £7 a unit in total. This gives a net cash inflow of £3 per unit sold (£10 - £7 = £3). The annual net cash flows to Cooper & Stone, i.e. cash receipts minus cash payments for business sales, can be thought of as the net profit before depreciation is calculated, and to this the initial cost of the machine and the final year proceeds from the machine sale are added to give all of the cash flows for the investment opportunity.

Depreciation is not included in the following table of cash flows and is calculated separately. The machine's original cost is £100,000, and at the end of the five years it can be sold for £25,000. The total deprecation is therefore £100,000 - £25,000 = £75,000, and assuming straight-line depreciation, where it is equal over each of the five years, the annual depreciation charge will therefore be £75,000 / 5 = £15,000.

Time	Source	Cash flow (£ 000s)
Immediately	Cost of machine	-100
1 year ahead	Net profit before depreciation (£3 x 10,000)	30
2 years ahead	Net profit before depreciation (£3 x 15,000)	45
3 years ahead	Net profit before depreciation (£3 x 20,000)	60
4 years ahead	Net profit before depreciation (£3 x 20,000)	60
5 years ahead	Net profit before depreciation (£3 x 5,000)	15
	Proceeds from machine sale	25

Annual average profit from the investment project before depreciation can be found from the table above, and the individual net profit before depreciation values must be totalled and averaged. This gives (30 + 45 + 60 + 60 + 15) = £210,000 total over the five years, and £210,000 / 5 = £42,000 average annual profit before depreciation. Taking away the annual depreciation charge gives £42,000 - £15,000 = £27,000 average annual profit from the investment.

The only other piece of information required to perform the ARR calculation is the average investment. A £100,000 investment for the purchase of the machine will of course be included in this total, but some may find it a surprise that the forecasted £25,000 cash proceeds from the sale of the same machine five years into the future at the end of the project is also included. It may appear more logical to include the resell value of the machine as part of the profit, instead of as an investment, but closer examination will reveal why this is not the case.

Investment may be seen as an opportunity cost, where the selection of the investment option costs what other alternatives, such as holding on to the money, could have offered in its place. Just as buying the machine in the first place has an opportunity cost of £100,000, the holding on to it for five years has an opportunity cost of £25,000 that could have always been made in resale. These two investments give an average investment of (£100,000 + £25,000) / 2 = £62,500.

$$\text{ARR} = (\text{Average annual profit} / \text{average investment}) \times 100\%$$
$$= (£27,000 / £62,500) \times 100\%$$
$$= 43.2\%$$

To decide whether the investment project should go ahead, this relatively high ARR of 43.2% would be compared to the minimum return rate required by the Cooper & Stone manufacturing business. If the minimum rate was higher then the project is no good, but if the ARR found here exceeds the rate then it may be selected to proceed unless an alternative machine investment under consideration offered an even higher ARR, while maintaining the same standards.

Example 2: TKMC

TKMC, a successful delivery business, is assessing the possibility of an investment in twelve new delivery vans, to transport products to its customers. The cost of each van is £15,000, and this must be paid right away, while annual running costs are expected to be £21,000 for each van, which includes the salaries for the drivers. All of the vans are expected to operate efficiently for six years, and after this period they will have to be sold, with the disposal value thought to be about £2,500 per van. The business currently uses a commercial carrier to make all of its deliveries, and the carrier is expected to charge £288,000 a year for the next six years on average. This means the vans would potentially save the business £288,000 - (£21,000 x 12) = £288,000 - £252,000 = £36,000 per year.

The annual cash inflows and outflows are given in the following table.

Time	Source	Cash flow (£ 000s)
Immediately	Cost of vans	-180
1 year ahead	Net saving before depreciation	36
2 years ahead	Net saving before depreciation	36
3 years ahead	Net saving before depreciation	36
4 years ahead	Net saving before depreciation	36
5 years ahead	Net saving before depreciation	36
6 years ahead	Net saving before depreciation	36
	Proceeds from van sale (12 x £2,500)	30

Depreciation here would be the cost of the vans at the beginning of the project, minus their value at the end. As shown above the vans cost £180,000 at the start of the six year period, and are worth £30,000 at the end. £180,000 - £30,000 = £150,000 depreciation in total, and assuming straight-line depreciation for six years this gives £150,000 / 6 = £25,000 annual depreciation charge.

Annual average profit before depreciation will be given by the savings before depreciation shown above, and the money saved in costs each year through the investment in the vans is essentially a profit. Normally the average would be found by totalling the income inflows for the individual years, and then dividing this by the number of years the investment project lasts. But here this doesn't need to be done as the profit before depreciation is the same each year, and the average is the same at £36,000. Taking away the annual depreciation charge of £25,000 gives £36,000 - £25,000 = £11,000 average annual profit.

There are two investments in the project, and the cost of the vans at £180,000 is the first, while example 1 above explained why the £30,000 resale value from selling the vans six years into the future must be included as an investment too. These two investments give an average investment of (£180,000 + £30,000) / 2 = £210,000 / 2 = £105,000.

$$\text{ARR} = (\text{Average annual profit} / \text{average investment}) \times 100\%$$
$$= (£11,000 / £105,000) \times 100\%$$
$$= 10.48\%$$

This is a modest rate of return for the investment, but still a positive one. The TKMC firm may or may not go ahead with the project, depending on their minimum target ARR, but with an ARR so low it would be unlikely.

Example 3: Chain Superstore

A chain of superstores is considering the purchase of a commercial property to expand its brand influence and increase sales. The firm has found a building that may be a suitable space, and it's priced at £200,000 which must be paid immediately. And the building would also require another £40,000 to cover the unavoidable renovation and branding costs. This makes a total initial investment of £200,000 + £40,000 = £240,000. If the superstore chain goes ahead with the proposed investment opportunity then it has forecast the new store to be potentially lucrative, and after a few years to build up its reputation in the local area this store should offer the same cash flows as the brand's others.

The investment project would be set to last for five years, after which the local store will be assessed again to determine whether or not it has met expectations, and the management will decide if the project should be continued or brought to an end. If it's sold then the £200,000 value of the building could be recovered, but the £40,000 renovation and branding costs would be lost forever as the new owners wouldn't want the branding, and it could be seen as a type of depreciation cost. The store's net cash flows from customers for each year are expected to be: £25,000 after one year; £35,000 after two years; £90,000 after three years; £95,000 after four years; and £95,000 after five years. All of this information can be summarized in a table to make the numbers and analysis clearer, in preparation for calculating the ARR.

Time	Source	Cash flow (£ 000s)
Immediately	Cost of building and renovation	-240
1 year ahead	Net profit before depreciation	25
2 years ahead	Net profit before depreciation	35
3 years ahead	Net profit before depreciation	90
4 years ahead	Net profit before depreciation	95
5 years ahead	Net profit before depreciation	95
	Proceeds from building sale	200

The average annual profit before depreciation is again given by the total of the yearly net profits divided by the number of years the investment lasts, and this equals (25 + 35 + 90 + 95 + 95) = £340,000 total over five years, for £340,000 / 5 = £68,000 average annual profit before depreciation. Depreciation is given by the decline in value of the investment over its life, £240,000 - £200,000 =

£40,000 total depreciation, and £40,000 / 5 = £8,000 annual depreciation costs. £68,000 - £8,000 = £60,000 average annual profit from the investment.

This project has two investments, with the initial building and renovation cost of £240,000, and opportunity cost of building sale proceeds at the end of the investment at £200,000. The total investment cost is £240,000 + £200,000 = £440,000, and £440,000 / 2 = £220,000 average investment.

$$ARR = (\text{Average annual profit} / \text{average investment}) \times 100\%$$
$$= (£60,000 / £220,000) \times 100\%$$
$$= 27.27\%$$

This is quite a healthy return and the decision on approval or rejection would again depend upon the minimum target ARR and how available alternatives compared.

Example 4: SpickSpan

SpickSpan, a growing cleaning company, have been offered a contract to maintain several important government buildings over the next four years. A government department has promised a set annual payment of £70,000 for the cleaning services, and SpickSpan would require an investment in new workers and cleaning equipment in order to meet the increased workload. Three new cleaners will be enough and each are available at a cost of £21,000 per year (3 x £21,000) = £63,000 a year in new salaries, while the cleaning project also involves ongoing product costs of £2,000 a year, and £63,000 + £2,000 = £65,000 annual project costs. This gives a net annual profit before depreciation of £70,000 - £65,000 = £5,000.

The project will also require an initial investment of £10,000 for new cleaning equipment including vacuum cleaners, and after four years of heavy use the equipment is thought to have a resale value of £2,000. All of this information is summarized in the table below.

Time	*Source*	*Cash flow (£ 000s)*
Immediately	Cost of cleaning equipment	-10
1 year ahead	Net profit before depreciation	5
2 years ahead	Net profit before depreciation	5
3 years ahead	Net profit before depreciation	5
4 years ahead	Net profit before depreciation	5
	Proceeds from equipment sale	2

Depreciation for the four year investment project is £10,000 - £2,000 = £8,000, and this gives £8,000 / 4 = £2,000 annual depreciation charge. This ensures an average annual investment profit after depreciation of £5,000 - £2,000 = £3,000.

There are two investments for this project, with the £10,000 cost of cleaning equipment the first, and the resale value opportunity cost of £2,000 the second. This gives an average investment of (£10,000 + £2,000) = £12,000 / 2 = £6,000. This figure and the average annual profit is all that's needed to find this project's ARR.

$$ARR = (\text{Average annual profit} / \text{average investment}) \times 100\%$$
$$= (£3,000 / £6,000) \times 100\%$$
$$= 50\%$$

A 50% annual rate of return is quite impressive, especially after only a four year investment project, and the SpickSpan company may be likely to take up the government contract if is assesses investment projects with the ARR method.

2.3 Problems with ARR

Although the four extended examples above haven't directly revealed it, the ARR method of evaluating investment opportunities suffers a major flaw that could lead investors to select a suboptimal investment. This problem can be found by modifying some of the information in the table above for SpickSpan.

The two areas classed as investments, the cost of cleaning equipment for SpickSpan and the proceeds from their sale after four years, will be unchanged at £-10,000 and £2,000 respectively, but the numbers given for the net profits before depreciation will be changed for each year. Originally this was £5,000 for each of the four years to give a £20,000 total, and a £5,000 average annual profit before depreciation. Minus annual depreciation of £2,000 gave a £3,000 average annual profit, before dividing by the £6,000 average investment meant an ARR of 50%.

But now two alternative cash flows will be created for the four year period; alternative A and alternative B. These two alternatives give different cash flows over the four year life of the investment project to the original example with SpickSpan. However, the cash flows for alternative A still total £20,000 just as before, again giving an annual average of £5,000. And exactly the same is true for alternative B, as the sum of the four years' cash flows is £20,000, and the average is £5,000. Just as with the example above, after depreciation of £2,000 per year these alternatives give £3,000 average annual profit, and dividing by the £6,000 average investment equals an ARR of 50%.

Alternative A cash flows (£ 000s)

1 year ahead = 2
2 years ahead = 2
3 year ahead = 2
4 years ahead = 14

Alternative B cash flows (£ 000s)

1 year ahead = 14
2 years ahead = 2
3 year ahead = 2
4 years ahead = 2

The problem revealed here is that ARR almost completely ignores the factor of time, and it doesn't account for the fact that money received sooner is more valued than the same amount of money received at a later date. Although alternatives A and B change the spread of the cash inflows over the investment period the ARR result remains the same as the total of the cash flows is unchanged. As far as the ARR is concerned the spread of the cash flows doesn't matter, and getting £2,000 after one year and £14,000 after four years in alternative A is just as good as £14,000 after one year and £2,000 after four years in alternative B. Yet if any investor was offered this choice they would all prefer alternative B without exception. This second alternative offers an extra £12,000 after one year compared to alternative A, and this could of course be invested in another project or at the very least saved in a bank for interest to generate significant profits and greater wealth. The fact that ARR doesn't distinguish between the original example, alternative A, and alternative B should be a major concern for those considering its use.

The ARR method can also cause problems when the competing investments under consideration are of a different size. Suppose a company is thinking over the purchase of a piece of land that will be used for a lucrative development. Option one has a capacity of 600,000 square metres, and is expected to produce an average profit of £3.6 million a year for the foreseeable future, although it requires a one-off investment of £9 million. Option two has a smaller capacity of 400,000 square metres, and is expected to offer an average profit of £3 million a year, although it requires an average investment of £6 million. For option one the ARR is £3,600,000 / £9,000,000 = 40%. For option two the ARR is £3,000,000 / £6,000,000 = 50%. Therefore option two has the higher ARR value here, and an investor judging solely on this investment appraisal measure would undoubtedly pick option two. However, if the absolute profit on offer from each of the two options is examined then it's clearly option one that's the winner, as its average profit is £3.6 million a year compared to £3 million a year for option two.

In reality most businesses are looking to maximize their profit in absolute terms and not relative ones. They aim to make as much wealth as possible, not just achieve a high rate of return for a modest investment. Therefore a firm may find that going against the ARR suggestion, and choosing option A over option B, may better suit their objectives. This is a problem with using comparative methods such as ARR or other percentage measures, when the stated goal of wealth generation is measured in absolute terms. And the problem with using a comparative measure can rear itself again even if one investment opportunity is far better than another. There is still the issue of comparing the investment's ARR with the minimum target ARR, and the selection of this target is completely arbitrary. An investment opportunity can be judged good or bad based on nothing whatsoever to do with its own characteristics, and simply because of the minimum rate of return desired by an investor.

Another problem with the ARR or ROCE method is that cash flows are usually more important than accounting profits for investment appraisal purposes. Cash is the truest measure of wealth generated, as cash is used to acquire needed resources and must be distributed to a firm's shareholders. Accounting profit as measured by the ARR or ROCE is more appropriate for reporting the short-term performance of a business, and although a useful measure to show the productive effort over a period of a year, its use diminishes over longer periods. For example, most businesses would want the resale value of an investment to be high, as that gives greater cash inflow, but as the ARR measure sees the resale as a separate investment a higher value would actually reduce the ARR, as greater profit would be sacrificed by not selling it sooner. A business could reject an investment project due to having a low ARR, when a large cause of the low return was a high investment resale value, something the business would actually prefer.

3 Payback Period (PP)

3.1 Payback Period Explained

The payback period (PP) method of investment appraisal appears to offer a solution to the problems caused by ARR ignoring the timing of cash flows. PP gives the length of time taken, usually in years, for the original investment to be paid back from the investment project's net cash flows.

For example, the initial investment for a project may be £60,000, which must be paid right away, with net cash flow profits expected to be £20,000 per year for four years, again paid at year end as assumed in previous examples. The cumulative net cash flows can then be calculated for each year to find the payback period:

<u>Cumulative cash flows (£ 000s)</u>

Now = -60
1 year ahead = -60 (+20) = -40
2 years ahead = -40 (+20) = -20
3 years ahead = -20 (+20) = 0
4 years ahead = 0 (+20) = 20

This project has a payback period of 3 years, and after this length of time the initial investment of £60,000 will have been paid off, which is shown by the net cash flow no longer being negative. When the net cash flows are the same for every year there's also an easier way to find the PP, and the initial investment simply has to be divided by the annual cash flow, and then rounded up to the next whole number. In this case £60,000 / £20,000 = 3 year payback period, as confirmed by the yearly results above.

If the initial investment was £100,000 and the annual cash flow was £19,000 then the payback period result would be £100,000 / £19,000 = 5.263 years to three decimal places, rounded up to give a 6 year payback period. If a precise PP was required, given in terms smaller than years, then in months it would be (£100,000 / £19,000) x 12 (months in a year) = 63.158 months, or 64 months if rounded up, for 5 years and 4 months. If the precise payback period was wanted in days then the 12 above would be replaced by the number of days in a year, which may be 365 for a non-leap year, 366 for a leap year, 365.25 to be precise, or 360 days as often used in financial markets or in computer models.

However, in real life the cash flows may not be the same for each year. In such a scenario the quick calculations above will not work and the only way to calculate the payback period will be cumulatively by year. Suppose there's another investment opportunity being considered, and it involves an initial investment of £250,000 that would generate a cash stream for ten years. The opportunity is expected to generate net profits of £40,000 for the first year; £60,000 for the second year; £110,000 for the third year; £80,000 for the fourth year; £75,000 for the fifth year; £90,000 each for years six and seven; £70,000 for year eight; £45,000 for year nine; and finally £20,000 for year ten. These are summarized in the table below, with a cumulative cash flow.

Cumulative cash flows (£ 000s)

Now = -250
1 year ahead = -250 (+40) = -210
2 years ahead = -210 (+60) = -150
3 years ahead = -150 (+110) = -40
4 years ahead = -40 (+80) = 40
5 years ahead = 40 (+75) = 115
6 years ahead = 115 (+90) = 205
7 years ahead = 205 (+90) = 295
8 years ahead = 295 (+70) = 365
9 years ahead = 365 (+45) = 410
10 years ahead = 410 (+20) = 430

The initial investment is £250,000 and after one year the cumulative cash flow remains negative at £-210,000. After two years it has become £-150,000 and once three years have passed it's £-40,000, which still shows an overall loss in the account of the business. But four years after the initial investment the business has finally rid itself of a negative cumulative cash flow, as it stands at £40,000. This gives a payback period of 4 years. And as the cumulative cash flow stood at £-40,000 after three years, and at £40,000 after four years, it's clear that the precise payback period is 3.5 years in this example.

Once the PP has been found an investor needs to decide if it's acceptable, and they would usually have a minimum payback period in mind before considering the investment opportunities. If the calculated PP was longer than this then the associated project may be rejected, but if it wasn't then it could go ahead. For example, if the minimum PP chosen by an investor was three years then the project just examined would be rejected as payback takes three and a half years here. But if the minimum payback period selected before opportunity evaluation was instead four years then the project may go ahead. In the situation where two or more competing projects both meet the minimum PP, then the investor should choose the opportunity with the shorter PP.

The payback period approach is very easy and low cost to use and calculate, and it can be understood easily by any financial manager. The appeal of using a PP is that it's associated with a more economically attractive selection, as projects that can recover their costs quickly are preferred to those with longer payback periods, to support liquidity and maintain the availability of a firm's assets.

3.2 Payback Period Extended Examples

With the process of calculating the payback period given above the method can now be applied further. It's useful to work through more examples that go into greater depth, and giving the specific details of the investment projects under consideration is more relevant to real life scenarios that only giving numbers with no background to base it on. The four examples here are again for Cooper & Stone, TKMC, the chain superstore, and SpickSpan, as they will be for all four investment appraisal methods to allow a comparison to be made.

Example 1: Cooper & Stone

As in the last chapter, the first extended payback period example relates to the manufacturing business Cooper & Stone, where the firm was considering an investment in a machine to develop a new sector of the business. This machine costs £100,000 to buy, and it should last for five years before depreciation greatly reduces its functionality, after which it could be sold for £25,000. If the investment was made then net profits could be expected of £30,000 in year one; £45,000 in year two;

£60,000 each in years three and four; and £15,000 in year five. This data is summarized again in the table below, along with the cumulative cash flow for the Cooper & Stone firm.

Time	Source	Cumulative Cash Flow (000s)
Immediately	Cost of machine	-100
1 year ahead	Net profit before depreciation (£3 x 10,000)	+30 = -70
2 years ahead	Net profit before depreciation (£3 x 15,000)	+45 = -25
3 years ahead	Net profit before depreciation (£3 x 20,000)	+60 = 35
4 years ahead	Net profit before depreciation (£3 x 20,000)	+60 = 95
5 years ahead	Net profit before depreciation (£3 x 5,000)	+15 = 110
	Proceeds from machine sale	+25 = 135

The payback period for this investment project is 3 years, and after this period the investment will pay for itself instead of using up the firm's cash reserves. To be more precise the PP is a little less than 2.5 years, and after two years the cumulative cash flow stands at £-25,000, while after three years it's at £35,000. But because it's usually assumed that payments are made at the end of the year, the fact that less than half of the year's net profits were needed to finish repaying the initial investment is irrelevant, and the payback period would be rounded up to the nearest year for a figure of 3 years. If it was instead assumed that cash flows arose evenly throughout the year then the precise PP would need to be calculated, by dividing the cash flow at the end of year two, £-25,000, by year three's net profit of £60,000. This gives £-25,000 / £60,000 = 0.41667, for a payback period of 2.41667 years.

Example 2: TKMC

The second extended example calculating the payback period will take another look at the TKMC business first seen earlier. The delivery business was considering an investment in a fleet of twelve new vans to transport its products to customers. Each of the twelve vans had a cost of £15,000 (£180,000 total), annual running costs were £21,000 for each van (£252,000 total), and the vans would replace a commercial carrier that cost £288,000 a year, giving a potential annual saving or profit of £36,000. The investment project and vans should have a working life of six years, and then they could be sold for £2,500 each (£30,000 total).

The data in the table shows that the initial investment will be paid back to the business after 5 years with the cumulative cash flow, and 5 years exactly is the payback period here.

Time	Source	Cumulative Cash Flow (000s)
Immediately	Cost of vans	-180
1 year ahead	Net saving pre depreciation	+36 = -144
2 years ahead	Net saving pre depreciation	+36 = -108
3 years ahead	Net saving pre depreciation	+36 = -72
4 years ahead	Net saving pre depreciation	+36 = -36
5 years ahead	Net saving pre deperciation	+36 = 0
6 years ahead	Net saving pre depreciation	+36 = 36
	Proceeds from van sale (12 x £2,500)	+30 = 66

Whether that is acceptable will depend entirely on TKMC and what they require. Something that may be a factor in their decision is the fact that the net saving here is expected to be the same for every year. This means that cash flows are thought to be relatively predictable, and therefore the calculated PP should also be more reliable. In other cases where the cash flows are expected to vary for each year the forecasts are more likely to be off, as the combination of factors giving that precise annual profit are expected to change for each year, and they could therefore change a little earlier or later than planned. This would cause the real payback period to differ from the predicted one, but fortunately for TKMC it's not an issue here.

Example 3: Chain Superstore

The third example looks at the chain superstore, which was considering the purchase of a commercial property to expand its business. The building comes at a price of £200,000, and £40,000 in renovation and branding costs would also be required, for £240,000 total investment costs. It's expected to generate increasing cash flows over the following five years, with £25,000 after one year; £35,000 after year two; £90,000 after year three; £95,000 after year four; and £95,000 after year five. And after the five year investment period the building can be sold for £200,000.

As the table shows the payback period is 4 years in this example, or to be more precise just under four years. After 3 years have passed after the initial investment the cumulative cash flow is still negative and the business is at a loss. But after year four ends the cumulative cash flow stands at £5,000, and the firm reports a gain from the investment. This may or may not be soon enough for the investor considering the project, depending on the predetermined minimum target, and if the goal was to quickly recoup the investment costs then the project may be rejected.

Time	Source	Cumulative Cash Flow (000s)
Immediately	Cost of building and renovation	-240
1 year ahead	Net profit before depreciation +25 =	-215
2 years ahead	Net profit before depreciation +35 =	-180
3 years ahead	Net profit before depreciation +90 =	-90
4 years ahead	Net profit before depreciation +95 =	5
5 years ahead	Net profit before depreciation +95 =	100
	Proceeds from building sale +200 =	300

An interesting thing about the PP method of investment appraisal is that it doesn't care about the total cash flows and profits, only the time it takes to pay off the initial investment. The huge profits in year five, including £200,000 on offer from the resale of the building investment to give a final cumulative cash flow of £300,000, are not relevant at all here because they occur after the payback period. This example reveals the PP method of investment appraisal to be primarily a short-term approach.

Example 4: SpickSpan

The fourth example involves cleaning company SpickSpan which was considering a four year government contract that would require an investment of £10,000 for cleaning equipment, but this would generate annual payments from government of £70,000. From this annual revenue an annual cost is subtracted to the value of £65,000, comprising £63,000 in salaries of £21,000 for three workers, and £2,000 for annual product costs. After the four year investment project ends the cleaning equipment's value is expected to have depreciated to £2,000.

Time	Source		Cumulative Cash Flow (000s)
Immediately	Cost of cleaning equipment		-10
1 year ahead	Net profit before depreciation	+5 =	-5
2 years ahead	Net profit before depreciation	+5 =	0
3 years ahead	Net profit before depreciation	+5 =	5
4 years ahead	Net profit before depreciation	+5 =	10
	Proceeds from equipment sale	+2 =	12

The payback period here is exactly 2 years, a short payback period which may make this investment project appealing to the SpickSpan company. Another factor working in the favour of this project is that the annual cash flows of £5,000 will come from a government contract. If cash flows came from another firm or from consumer sales then there's a risk that these groups may find themselves in financial trouble and be unable to pay, or simply bad firms or problematic consumers who refuse to honour the terms of their agreement. But with a government contract the risk that the expected cash flows don't come to pass are gone, as government will both be the last group to run into financial trouble, and are also likely to be the most predictable and reliable group to deal with.

3.3 Problems with Payback Period

Although payback period does take time into consideration, which was a major flaw of ARR and the use of the accounting rate for return as a measure of investment evaluation, it comes with its own flaws. This was suggested in the last section and can be shown further with another example. The cash flows linked with four more hypothetical investments are given below:

<u>Cash flows for investment opportunity A (£ 000s)</u>

Initial investment now = -100
Net cash flow after 1 year = 30
Net cash flow after 2 years = 30
Net cash flow after 3 years = 40
Net cash flow after 4 years = 30
Net cash flow after 5 years = 30
Disposal value after 5 years = 20

<u>Cash flows for investment opportunity B (£ 000s)</u>

Initial investment now = -100
Net cash flow after 1 year = 10

Net cash flow after 2 years = 10
Net cash flow after 3 years = 80
Net cash flow after 4 years = 5
Net cash flow after 5 years = 5
Disposal value after 5 years = 10

Cash flows for investment opportunity C (£ 000s)

Initial investment now = -100
Net cash flow after 1 year = 10
Net cash flow after 2 years = 30
Net cash flow after 3 years = 60
Net cash flow after 4 years = 200
Net cash flow after 5 years = 500
Disposal value after 5 years = 20

Cash flows for investment opportunity D (£ 000s)

Initial investment now = -100
Net cash flow after 1 year = 25
Net cash flow after 2 years = 25
Net cash flow after 3 years = 50
Net cash flow after 4 years = 0
Net cash flow after 5 years = 0
Disposal value after 5 years = 0

In all four investment opportunities here the initial investment is £100,000. Most importantly, and the only significant factor as far as PP is concerned, is that all four take the same time of three years for this original investment to be recovered. Opportunity A is expected to produce (30 + 30 + 40) over the three years; opportunity B is forecast to offer (10 + 10 + 80) over years one to three; investment opportunity C is expected to give cash flows (10 + 30 + 60) over the same three year period; and finally investment D will give cash flows (25 + 25 + 50) over these three years. So as far as the payback period of investment appraisal method is concerned all four projects are of equal value, and all are equally as good at paying back the £100,000 invested in as quick a time as possible.

However, no investor would judge the projects equally, and opportunity C would be their clear preference without exception, while opportunity D is the one they would all avoid. Investment opportunity A offers (30 + 30 + 20) = 80 thousand over years four and five, opportunity B is expected to give (5 + 5 + 10) = 20 thousand over the same period, opportunity C will make (200 + 500 + 20) = 720 thousand over years four and five, and finally opportunity D will make (0 + 0 + 0) = 0 thousand (i.e. nothing) over years four and five. But because the payback period measure doesn't care what happens after the initial investment costs are paid back, the events of years four and five don't matter. Cash flows outside the payback period are ignored, and this is inconsistent with wealth maximization, the stated goal of any business.

Using PP to evaluate investments may be seen as a strategy to manage risk, as by selecting the project with the shortest time taken to pay back costs, there may appear to be less risk that those costs won't be paid back. But there are many individual areas of risk to be managed, and a crude strategy based on a rushed attempt to recover costs is unlikely to be the best way to address them. Add in the fact that the choice of minimum payback period to measure the PP of projects against is completely arbitrary, and PP seems to be a problematic approach.

ARR was flawed as an investment appraisal measure because it ignored the time value of money, where money is more valuable if received sooner, but PP only addresses this in a very crude way. Here money is valuable if received 'soon enough' for a targeted minimum payback period, but worthless and ignored if received after this. And within this payback period the time value of money is again completely ignored, just as with the ARR, and no distinction is made between paying back most (e.g. 90%) of the investment costs in the first year of a certain payback period, or most (e.g. 90% again) only in the final year. Yet all investors would undoubtedly prefer the former, as the money would then be available to invest in something else.

An alternative investment appraisal method is needed which takes all of an investment's cash flows into account, unlike payback period, but which also makes an allowance for the effects of the timing of those cash flows.

4 Net Present Value (NPV)

4.1 NPV Explained

To overcome the problems found with the previous two investment appraisal methods, a measure is required that: takes all of the costs and benefits of each investment opportunity into account; and notes the distinct effects of the timings of those costs and benefits. The net present value (NPV) method meets these criteria, and represents a discounted cash flow (DCF) method of investment appraisal. With NPV all cash flows are discounted by the effect that time is expected to have on their value.

Cash flows need to be discounted in order to represent their true value, as £100 today is worth more than £100 a year from now. No-one would be prepared to sacrifice £100 now to receive the same amount a year in the future for three separate reasons; interest lost; risk; and inflation effects.

Interest lost affects the value of money over time, and if a sum of money is kept out of our hands for a year, then not only has the opportunity to spend the money been taken away, but so has the opportunity to save and put it in a bank. If this option was chosen then a year from now the saver would still have the original amount, and a sum of interest would be added to it too. Unless money invested in a project matches the interest return that could have been made if it was put in a bank, then the investor is suffering an opportunity cost, where the investment project has deprived him of the opportunity to make the returns available from savings interest. And in reality the investment project must offer a better return on an investor's money than a bank, or he would simply forego the investment and put the money in a bank to claim the same return through interest, without all of the effort that undertaking the investment project would involve.

Risk is another factor, and an investment project is only based on what those making the investment expect to happen, and the cash flows they forecast will be paid and received over certain timeframes. But all of these calculations and estimates are made before the investment is made, and there's a risk that things won't go as planned. Looking at the Cooper & Stone manufacturing business example used earlier, a number of things could go wrong with the machine project they were considering investing in. The machine may not function as expected, and it could break down to halt the new business service and the associated sales and profits. Even if the machine works as planned, the service may not generate the cash flows that were forecast, as estimated sales may not materialize to reduce cash inflows, or labour costs paid to employees may end up higher than thought to cause greater cash outflows. And a final possible problem may occur right at the end of the investment project, as the proceeds from the sale of the machine could be lower than predicted.

Because the investment in a new machine for their service sector is inherently risky for Cooper & Stone, the business would expect a higher return that offered a risk premium over the return they could achieve with no risk at all, such as putting the money in a bank to gain interest. The precise level of the risk premium excess return, relative to the risk-free return available from savings interest, would be decided based on the amount of risk that is thought to be associated with a project.

Inflation can't be ignored, and if an individual is deprived of a sum of money for a year, then by the time it comes to spending it the sum of money will buy less than it would have done a year earlier. Prices follow a trend of rising over time, and this price inflation means that the purchasing power for a sum of money will fall the further into the future it is received. To make up for this an individual would expect a higher sum of money if it's to be received in the future, to match the purchasing power that would have been achieved if the amount of money had been received in the present. This addition would be on top of the increase in return demanded in order to account for the risk of the project. In practice market interest rates usually account for inflation, and those putting their money in a bank will typically get a rate that allows for higher prices in the future, and makes an attempt to adjust for purchasing power parity.

Putting the three time-related factors together, a rational and logical investor who intends to increase his wealth will only invest in projects which compensate for the loss of interest and purchasing power of the money invested in the opportunities, while also covering the possibility and risk that the expected returns will not arrive. A return set at the same level as market interest rates would cover the loss of interest, and because these rates make an allowance for inflation they would also compensate for that issue. The only factor still to be addressed would be risk, and a risk premium additional return would need to be added to the market rate of interest to give what could be called an opportunity rate, or more commonly a discount rate, which accounts for all the opportunity costs of an investment. One way to determine this rate would be to find an investment with a similar level of risk at the one being considered, and find the rate of return linked to it. For example, a business could investigate other firms who have already been through a similar investment project, and average out the returns that they received. Adjusting this for yearly returns could give an opportunity rate.

While the appropriate discount rate to use during NPV analysis would be the opportunity cost of the investment opportunity, and the return rate linked with the best alternative that would have to be foregone as a result, this isn't always known. Even if it is, it isn't necessarily the case that firms have money lying around that they would have invested in an alternative opportunity. Perhaps if a certain investment wasn't found to be worthwhile then the firm wouldn't have invested in anything, and it wouldn't have raised the cash together to fund it. As a result the discount rate for a project can also be known as the opportunity cost of finance, and it represents the cost to the business of the finance which would be used to fund the investment, if it went ahead. This will usually be the cost of the combination of funds used by the firm, including shareholders' funds and borrowed money, and is normally known as the cost of capital. In the event that an opportunity rate can't be found to use as the discount rate, then the cost of capital may be used instead.

Once the discount rate (R) (cost of capital or opportunity rate) has been found it can be used to adjust future cash flows to their present value (PV). The cash flow (CF) for each year would be recorded, and then discounted to its true present value using the discount rate, and the number of years (N) ahead that the cash flow was due to be received, with the following formula:

PV of CF in year N = actual cash flow in year N divided by $(1 + R)^N$

This formula works both ways, and it can also used to find future cash flows if the relevant factors are known. For example, a business may have been offered a 20% return per year (R = 0.2) for taking on a risky project. It could invest £1,000 today (year 0) in this project and after two years (N = 2) it would be expected to have earned:

$$£1,000 = (CF \text{ in year } 2) / (1 + 0.2)^2$$

This can be rearranged to make (CF in year 2) the subject, by multiplying both sides by $(1 + 0.2)^2$:

$$CF \text{ in year } 2 = £1,000 \times (1 + 0.2)^2$$
$$CF \text{ in year } 2 = £1,440$$

To prove the formula can be used to find the present value of future cash flows, we can now forget that the original sum invested was £1,000 and treat it as unknown. This sum of money should be able to be calculated, using only the future cash flow, the return rate, and the number of years of the investment:

$$\text{PV of CF in year 2} = £1,440 / (1 + 0.2)^2$$
$$\text{PV of CF in year 2} = £1,000$$

This confirms that the present value formula works as it should. And it shows that an investor would be indifferent between £1,000 now and £1,440 in two years, assuming that the investment opportunity return or discount rate is 20%.

The PV formula can now be used to evaluate all cash flows associated with an investment opportunity, to determine whether the investment is worth pursuing. For example, a firm may be considering an investment project that would last for 2 years. The safe market rate of interest the firm could get by putting the money in a bank is 2%, and the firm believes that after risk is taken into account a suitable discount rate for the project is 10% (a risk premium of 8%), as other similar risky investment opportunities are available that offer a return of 10% a year. If the investment is made by the firm then it would have to pay £100,000 immediately, and then cash flows are expected to be £40,000 in year one and £80,000 in year two.

The present value (PV) of the cash flows (CF) in £000s is as follows for each year, where $R = 10\% = 0.1$:

Immediately (Year 0)

$$CF = -100$$
$$PV = -100 / (1 + 0.1)^0 = -100$$

Anything raised to the power zero is 1, and this removes the bracketed part of the equation here.

Year 1

$$CF = 40$$
$$PV = 40 / (1 + 0.1)^1 = 36.36$$

Year 2

$$CF = 80$$
$$PV = 80 / (1 + 0.1)^2 = 66.12$$

The net present value (NPV) of the investment project is found by summing all of the individual PV results for each year, and this shows the project's value after the cash flows for all years have been discounted to give their true value:

$$NPV = -100 + 36.36 + 66.12 = 2.48$$

This project's net present value is roughly £2,480. This isn't a precise figure here as the constituent parts and PV values for each year were rounded up or down to 2 decimal places, but it's accurate to the nearest ten pounds sterling and this is close enough for the analysis here. For a more precise figure the discounted cash flows for each year would be summed without any rounding up or down to decimal places occurring first.

The calculated NPV value is judged on if it is positive or negative, and if NPV is negative (or zero) then the cash flows associated with the investment project will not generate a profit, and the opportunity is rejected. But if the NPV is positive then the project's cash flows will generate a profit, and the investment opportunity is accepted. In the scenario where two of more competing projects both have a positive NPV the project with the highest NPV will be chosen.

Turning back to the example just examined, it takes £100,000 to invest in the project and it will earn a positive NPV profit of £2,480. That means that the benefits of investing are worth £102,480 today, and come at a cost of just £100,000 today. The firm can therefore 'buy' £102,480 of benefits at a cost of £100,000, which is clearly a good deal and a sound investment. But if the NPV of this project had turned out as a negative number, then the benefits of the investment opportunity would be worth less than £100,000 in today's money as a present value. That means that under £100,000 of benefits would come at a cost of over £100,000 to 'buy', and in such a scenario the investment should be avoided as it's clearly not worth it.

4.2 NPV Using Discount Tables and Excel

The last section showed that the present value (PV) of a future year's cash flow (CF) can be found with the following formula, where R is the discount rate:

PV of CF in year N = actual cash flow in year N divided by $(1 + R)^N$

However, in practice this process can be laborious, and first the $(1 + R)^N$ part of the equation needs to figured out, before the relevant year's cash flow is divided by the result to give the present value of that year's cash flow. But there is a quicker way of adjusting a sum of money to be received in the future to its PV. There are tables that present the ready made discount factor results, $1 / (1 + R)^N$, for a range of values of N and R, and these discount factors can be multiplied by the corresponding year's cash flow to find the present value. These tables could be created from scratch quite easily, but then that itself would be a laborious process, and creating a table of all the possible discount factors would take even more effort than just calculating them as required. Therefore it's useful to find ready made discount tables, and these are often given in an appendix of business textbooks, or they can be found freely over the internet.

The example used in the last section had a 10% discount rate, R = 0.1, and the investment project lasted for two years, which would give N = 1 in the first year, and N = 2 in the second. According to the discount tables, N = 1, R = 0.1 gives a discount factor of 0.909 to three significant figures, while N = 2, R = 0.1 gives a discount factor of 0.826, again to three significant figures. These would then be multiplied by the cash flows given for years one and two respectively to find their present value. The example from the previous section had cash flows of £40,000 in year one, and £80,000 in year two. Multiplying each by the discount factor to give the PV, gives £40,000 x 0.909 = £36,360 PV of year one's cash flow, and £80,000 x 0.826 = £66,080 PV of year two's cash flow. But while using the more laborious original method above also gave a PV of £36,360 for year one, the PV calculated for year two was £66,120, which represents a disparity.

The problem is that the values given in discount tables are not usually given in entirety, but rounded off to a number of significant figures, and this causes a disparity between the results that are found and the real ones. With this problem potentially replicated over multiple years of cash flows for an investment project, and with the size of the disparity increasing as larger sums of money are involved, there's a risk that the disparity between the real and calculated NPV could be sufficiently large to cause the wrong investment opportunity to be chosen.

Fortunately there's a way to avoid both the limited accuracy in using discount factors from ready made tables, and the work involved in calculating them ourselves. And that solution comes with Microsoft Excel. There's a very simple way to calculate the NPV of a project, and it will be explained step by step using the information from the example above once again. Remember that £100,000 was invested right away; the expected cash flow was £40,000 in year one and £80,000 in year two; and the investment opportunity return rate available on projects of a similar risk (i.e. the discount rate) was 10% or 0.1. To calculate the NPV of this investment opportunity the following steps must be taken in Excel:

Step 1: Open Excel.
Step 2: Select cell A1 and type '-100,000'.
Step 3: Select cell A2 and type '40,000'.
Step 4: Select cell A3 and type '80,000'.
Step 5: Select cell A1 again.
Step 6: Select 'Insert Function (fx)' on the toolbar. Holding shift and pressing F3 achieves the same goal.

Step 7: Change the category to 'Financial'.

Step 8: Scroll down the alphabetical list and select 'NPV'.

Step 9: Select OK.

Step 10: In the 'Rate' box type '0.1'.

Step 11: In the 'Value1' box type 'A2:A3'.

Step 12: Select OK.

Step 13: Look at cell A1, and the NPV of the project is given, at 2,479.34.

This process can be amended and simplified to show how to calculate the NPV of any project:

Step 1: In Excel select cell A1, and type the cost of the initial investment. This should have a negative sign in front of it to signal that it's a cost.

Step 2: In cell A2 type the cash flow expected in year one, in A3 type the cash flow expected in year two, in A4 type the cash flow expected in year three, etc., until all cash flows are represented in order in the A cells.

Step 3: Select cell A1, with the initial investment amount, and then select Insert Function (fx) on the toolbar (or hold shift and press F3), change to the Financial category, and scroll down to select NPV. It's essential that cell A1 containing the initial investment is selected before proceeding to find the NPV, and if it isn't then the result calculated will be incorrect.

Step 4: Type the discount rate into the Rate box, and in the Value1 box type the cells associated with all cash flows except for the initial investment, each separated with a colon ':' (A2:A3:A4 etc.). Select OK and the NPV of the project will appear in cell A1, replacing the initial investment.

4.3 NPV Extended Examples

The process of calculating NPV has been shown in the previous sections, and now it can be used to assess the two examples already examined with the ARR and Payback Period methods of investment appraisal.

<u>Example 1: Cooper & Stone</u>

Manufacturing firm Cooper & Stone is considering an investment in a machine that would expand its services and scope. The cash flows linked with this investment are given in the table below, with the present value of each year's cash flow given along with the overall NPV of the project. One factor added that wasn't seen when the example was looked at earlier is the discount rate. A standard discount rate of 10% is used and the discounted cash flow present value results are shown in the next table.

This project has a net present value of roughly £75,360 (Excel may give a slightly different result due to rounding as noted), and for an investment of £100,000 the firm Cooper & Stone can expect to achieve cash flows of £175,360 after five years. This is a positive high return and the NPV analysis suggests that this investment opportunity would be wealth generating and a good choice. While the analysis given by ARR and payback period appraisal methods didn't come to a firm conclusion on this project, the NPV adds a great deal of insight, and it suggests that Cooper & Stone would be well advised to invest in this opportunity and buy the machine. The only factor to note would be that this result is dependent on a discount rate of 10%, and the actual rate may be different in reality. With a significant variation between the discount rate calculated here and the real one the NPV result may be completely different, and it may be far higher or far lower and even negative. This will be explored further later in the book.

Time	*Source*	*Present value (000s)*
Immediately	Cost of machine	−100
1 year ahead	Net profit before depreciation (£3 x 10,000)	30 = 27.27
2 years ahead	Net profit before depreciation (£3 x 15,000)	45 = 37.19
3 years ahead	Net profit before depreciation (£3 x 20,000)	60 = 45.08
4 years ahead	Net profit before depreciation (£3 x 20,000)	60 = 40.98
5 years ahead	Net profit before depreciation (£3 x 5,000)	15 = 9.31
	Proceeds from machine sale	25 = 15.52
		NPV = 75.36

Example 2: TKMC

TKMC were looking at investing in twelve new vans to distribute their products to customers, which was expected to come at a lower cost than the commercial carrier currently being used. The associated cash flows are given again below, along with their present value assuming a discount rate of 10%, and the overall NPV of the project.

Time	Source	Present value (000s)
Immediately	Cost of vans	-180
1 year ahead	Net saving before depreciation	36 = 32.73
2 years ahead	Net saving before depreciation	36 = 29.75
3 years ahead	Net saving before depreciation	36 = 27.05
4 years ahead	Net saving before depreciation	36 = 24.59
5 years ahead	Net saving before depreciation	36 = 22.35
6 years ahead	Net saving before depreciation	36 = 20.32
	Proceeds from van sale (12 x £2,500)	30 = 16.93
	NPV =	-6.28

The investment project that TKMC has been evaluating has a negative NPV of £-6,280. Even with a huge investment of £180,000 the six year project is set to generate a loss instead of a profit here, and it should therefore be avoided. While ARR and payback methods suggested that this investment opportunity may have something to offer, NPV analysis conclusively suggests that this opportunity should not be considered under any circumstances, assuming a discount rate of 10% which is often the default used for projects.

Example 3: Chain Superstore

The chain superstore were considering an investment in a new building and renovation to create a new store to sell their products to consumers. The present value of the associated annual cash flows are given below along with the total net present value, assuming a 10% discount rate as with the other examples.

The chain superstore's investment project has an NPV of £127,330, and this is positive to ensure that the opportunity may be worth considering. However, most of this NPV only comes right at the end of the five year project with the sale of the building that was invested in, and the actual project itself appears to offer a relatively poor return. The chain superstore may still go ahead with the project but a £240,000 investment may be better spent elsewhere, and ironically the firm may be better off by simply buying the building for £200,000, forgetting about the renovation costs of £40,000, and then selling the building after holding on to it for five years. That may give an NPV almost as high but without all of the work that this project would involve.

Time	Source	Cash flow (£ 000s)
Immediately	Cost of building and renovation	-240
1 year ahead	Net profit before depreciation	25 = 22.73
2 years ahead	Net profit before depreciation	35 = 28.93
3 years ahead	Net profit before depreciation	90 = 67.62
4 years ahead	Net profit before depreciation	95 = 64.89
5 years ahead	Net profit before depreciation	95 = 58.99
	Proceeds from building sale	200 = 124.18
		NPV = 127.33

Example 4: SpickSpan

Cleaning company SpickSpan had been offered a four year government contract to service several government buildings. The associated cash flows are given again in the table that follows, along with the present value of each year's annual cash flow and the total net present value.

Time	Source	Cash flow (£ 000s)
Immediately	Cost of cleaning equipment	-10
1 year ahead	Net profit before depreciation	5 = 4.55
2 years ahead	Net profit before depreciation	5 = 4.13
3 years ahead	Net profit before depreciation	5 = 3.76
4 years ahead	Net profit before depreciation	5 = 3.42
	Proceeds from equipment sale	2 = 1.37
		NPV = 7.22

The NPV here is £7,220, and four years after investing £10,000 in the project the cleaning firm can expect to earn £17,220 back. The return of just £5,000 a year may have appeared poor at first, but this suggest otherwise. This is an impressive return of over 72% in just four years, and it comes at a cost of just a £10,000 original investment. This is further evidence that this is a good investment choice for SpickSpan, but the final decision will depend on their own circumstances.

Conclusions on Net Present Value

Although NPV analysis depends upon finding the correct discount rate, which could be a problem in certain circumstances, it seems to be a better method of investment appraisal overall than either the accounting rate of return (ARR) or payback period, and it addresses the main issues with them noted earlier. NPV takes full account of the timing of cash flows and discounts them according to the time they're expected to arrive; it includes all relevant cash flows for an investment project and each impacts on the overall investment decision; and it's aligned with the natural objectives of a business to maximize wealth. A positive NPV reveals a wealth creating opportunity and a negative NPV highlights a wealth reducing opportunity, and where a choice must be made between two projects the one with a higher NPV will create greater wealth, and should be chosen.

5 Internal Rate of Return (IRR)

5.1 IRR Explained

The final popular investment appraisal method to be examined is the internal rate of return (IRR). This is similar to the NPV method, and also follows a discounted cash flow (DCF) approach. The internal rate of return of an investment opportunity is the discount rate applied to future cash flows that generates an NPV of exactly zero, and in effect the IRR is the yield or rate of return of the project.

If the cash flows for an investment project were to give an NPV of £10,000 at a discount rate of 10%, then this means that the investment offers a rate of return for the business of over 10%, as with a discount rate at this level the present value of all of the cash flows combined is still positive. If the discount rate was increased to 20% and the NPV fell to £-10,000, then this means that the rate of the return on the investment is lower than 20%, as a discount rate at this level gives a negative overall cash flow. The results using 10% and 20% discount rates would suggest that the IRR, the discount rate giving an NPV of exactly zero, must lie somewhere between the two. Perhaps changing the discount rate to 15% would finally give an NPV of precisely £0 in this example, and if so this would mean the rate or return on the investment project is 15%. Because the IRR can't be calculated directly, due to its value depending entirely on the NPV of a project, the only approach to use is trial and error as here.

If the discount rate is zero then the NPV would simply be the sum of the project's net cash flows, and the time value of money would be completely ignored. But as the discount rate is increased the NPV of a project will decrease. Because the net cash flows of an investment project are likely to be positive before discounting to present value, or an investor wouldn't be tempted to even consider the investment opportunity in the first place, it can be a good strategy to start with a reasonable discount rate of roughly 10% when trying to find the IRR. This would usually give a positive NPV, and then this rate can be raised until the NPV approaches zero, at which point the changes made would become smaller until the exact value of zero NPV is reached.

A decision rule on the calculated IRR value would involve satisfying a minimum IRR requirement, similar to the ARR and payback period method examined earlier. This minimum target rate should logically be set at a level of the opportunity cost of finance (cost of capital), as this represents the firm's costs and if these aren't met then the firm will suffer a loss if it proceeds with the investment.

IRR has a great deal in common with NPV, which would be expected considering it's based around achieving a certain NPV value (zero). IRR takes all cash flows into account, while their timing is also dealt with properly as they're discounted according to the time of expected arrival.

5.2 IRR Extended Examples, IRR in Excel

IRR will be the final investment appraisal method to be applied to the four extended examples looked at earlier. The section on ARR introduced the cash flows of their investment projects for each year, as a basis to find the average annual profit and average investment to calculate the accounting rate of return. Payback period's analysis of the two firms' investment opportunities added a cumulative cash flow over time, which was used to find the period where the initial investment would be paid off. And most recently NPV gave the present value of the projects' cash flows by year, to allow an overall project present value to be calculated. But with IRR there's little more depth that can be added to the examples, as the process is based around simple trial and error. It would be a waste of time and space to repeat the whole present value discounting process used above multiple times, for different discount rates in a trial and error process.

The best and most efficient method to calculate a project's IRR is with Microsoft Excel. This also uses trial and error to find the rate of return where a project's NPV is equal to precisely zero, but it does it quickly and with no effort. The steps used to find the IRR with Excel are as follows:

Step 1: In Excel select cell A1, and type the cost of the initial investment. This should have a negative sign in front of it to signal that it's a cost.

Step 2: In cell A2 type the cash flow expected in year one, in A3 type the cash flow expected in year two, in A4 type the cash flow expected in year three, etc., until all cash flows are represented in order in the A cells.

Step 3: Select cell B1, with no numbers entered into it, and then select Insert Function (fx) on the toolbar, change to the Financial category, and scroll down to select IRR. It's essential that a blank cell such as B1 is selected before proceeding to find the IRR, and if it isn't then the process will not work properly.

Step 4: Type 0.1 (or any number you want, it makes no difference) into the Guess box, and in the Values box type the cells associated with all cash flows, including the initial investment, each separated with a colon ':' (A1:A2:A3:A4 etc.). No other cell values should be entered into the Values box except for all of those that contain the investment's cash flows. Select OK and the IRR of the project will appear in cell B1, the last selected cell. If you receive a warning popup that Excel can't calculate a formula because of a circular reference, or if the IRR value found is negative or zero, then either the steps haven't been followed properly, or there's a problem with the cash flows (see problems with IRR below).

With the procedure to find the IRR given above, the focus can move to a last look at the four extended examples used throughout this book, Cooper & Stone, TKMC, the chain superstore, and SpickSpan.

Example 1: Cooper & Stone

Cooper & Stone are a firm considering an investment in a machine to develop a service sector. The NPV analysis performed earlier predicted the investment would generate a profit, at £75,360 NPV using a discount rate of 10%. An NPV of zero is needed for the IRR and therefore the discount rate needs to be higher. Testing different discount rates quickly and easily in Excel shows that a rate of 20% gives a NPV of £35,980, and even using a very high discount rate of 30% still gives a positive NPV, at £8,790. This trend shows that the discount rate needs to be raised even higher to find the IRR, but not too much above 30%. Trying a 35% discount rate gives an NPV of £-1,720, and therefore a 35% discount rate is too high.

Using Excel's IRR method noted above the actual IRR is found to be 0.34127 or 34.127%. This means that Cooper & Stone can expect a yield of a little over 34% if they invest in the machine they have under consideration. To gain a rate of return of over a third is impressive and even without knowing more about the firm and its needs it seems likely that this machine would be a good investment.

Example 2: TKMC

TKMC are thinking over a possible investment in twelve new vans, to transport their products to customers at a lower cost. The NPV for a discount rate of 10% was calculated earlier and was found to be £-6,280. This negative number suggests that the discount rate is too high and it needs to fall a little, to raise the NPV and find the zero NPV that gives the IRR. If the discount rate were changed to 5% in Excel then the NPV would be £25,110, a positive amount that's far above the zero NPV that is the target. 5% is therefore too low, and the discount rate needs to be less than 10% but close to it.

Calculating the IRR in Excel with the method above reveals the actual IRR to be 0.088936 or 8.8936%. This means that TKMC should achieve a rate of return of almost 9% if they were to invest in the fleet of new transport vans. As this is quite low it may not be above their cost of capital, a pre-requisite for selecting an IRR, and if not then this investment opportunity should be avoided.

Example 3: Chain Superstore

A chain superstore are looking into a purchase and renovation of a building to create another branch of its stores. The NPV of this project was £127,330 with a 10% discount rate. This suggests that the discount rate isn't high enough, and a discount rate of 20% gives an NPV of £21,590, which is still above zero. A 30% discount rate gives an NPV of £-46,380, to suggest this is now too high a rate, and a 25% discount rate gives the NPV of £-15,940 to show that 25% is also too high a rate. The discount rate that would give an NPV of zero is clearly between 20 and 25%.

Using Excel to calculate the IRR as explained above gives a 0.22744 or 22.744% internal rate of return. This means that the chain superstore can expect a yield of almost 23% if it invests in the project under consideration. This is a relatively high yield and is likely to be above the firm's cost of capital, but a chain superstore as in this example may be used to earning greater returns than this and may expect a higher return, especially based on the significant sum of money of £240,000 that the investment will require.

Example 4: SpickSpan

The cleaning company SpickSpan have been offered a generous four year contract by a government department where they will gain £70,000 a year for servicing several state buildings, but they must first invest in associated cleaning equipment and would have worker and product costs each year too. The NPV for this project if a 10% discount rate is used is £7,220. This suggests the discount rate is too low and a higher rate is needed for the desired NPV of zero, to find the IRR and the yield of the project. A 20% discount rate gives a £3,910 NPV which is still too low, and even a 30% discount rate gives an NPV of £1,530. But a 40% rate is too high and will cause a negative NPV of £-230, yet a 35% discount rate is too low and gives a positive NPV of £590. The discount rate required to find the IRR is somewhere between 35% and 40%.

Using Excel to find the IRR directly gives a result of 38.507%, and the firm can expect a yield and return of not far under 40% from this investment project. To gain almost a 40% return after just a four year investment project is very impressive, and the best seen in all of these examples. Add in that this comes at a cost of just a £10,000 investment, with no risk due to the opportunity coming from a government contract, and it seems that this is an ideal project for SpickSpan.

5.3 Problems with IRR

IRR has much in common with NPV, and as a result it can be a useful tool as it can reveal the exact rate of return linked to an investment project. But it does suffer some problems. Like the accounting rate of return before it, the clue to one of these problems is given by the name of the internal rate of return, as IRR is only focused on the relative return and does not focus on wealth generation, the primary goal of any business. This can lead to the wrong decision being made during investment appraisal.

Judging investments solely on IRR would see a project with a 30% IRR always chosen over another project with only a 20% IRR, assuming that the opportunity cost of finance or cost of capital was lower, at say 15%. But while the project with a 30% rate of return may be the better option to increase wealth, this will not necessarily be the case, as the IRR method ignores the scale of an investment opportunity. For example, assuming a 15% opportunity cost of finance, a project involving a £10 million investment and offering a 20% return gives a 5% net return rate (20 - 15), and generates £500,000, while a project involving a £1 million investment for a 30% return rate gives a 15% net return rate (30 - 15), and generates only £150,000. As businesses aim to maximize profits the project with the lower 20% return would be preferred by firms, but IRR would advise against it here.

However, it's unusual for two projects of completely different scales and investment requirements to be competing with each other for a firm's approval, and as a result IRR can usually be relied upon to give the same signal as NPV. But if the project with the greater percentage return isn't the one with the higher cash flow profits then IRR will be a poor choice for firms, and it must be better to prefer NPV to IRR as it's always focused on wealth maximization, the goal of every firm. IRR can still be useful however, and despite its flaws in comparing different investments it can show whether a single project is worth investing in, giving the rate of return which can then be compared with the cost of capital.

Another problem with IRR is that it can struggle to deal with projects that have unnatural cash flows. The typical investment would have a negative cash flow at the start, with a large initial investment cost, and then a positive cash flow after this with smaller and slower return benefits in the following years. But it may be the case that an investment project's cash flows follow a different pattern, and later years can also have additional costs and overall negative cash flows. If this happens then there can be more than one discount rate that gives an NPV of zero, or alternatively the NPV may remain negative throughout and never equal zero. Either way, with two IRR values or none at all in certain circumstances, relying on the internal rate of return method of investment appraisal alone may not be an option.

6 Investment Appraisal in Practice

6.1 Potential Sources of Error

The previous sections have shown how investment appraisal is conducted, but there are several practical issues that should be kept in mind to avoid erroneous investment calculations and decisions.

Some opportunity costs can often be forgotten in investment appraisal, and when considering a new investment businesses should remember to take into account the cash flows available from selling the old assets. To avoid irrelevant factors confusing the analysis, only variable costs related to the investment decision should be taken into account, and fixed cash flows that will remain irrespective of the project chosen should be ignored.

Taxation levels will be affected by an investment decision, and huge profits will be taxed at a higher rate than lower returns, while certain types of investments may attract tax breaks. Effective investment appraisal will take note of exactly how alternative project choices will affect tax rates and net cash flows, and adjust the relevant calculations accordingly.

For the payback period, NPV and IRR methods the evaluation of projects depends upon cash flows and not profit flows. But in certain circumstances the only information available may be the investment's yearly income or profit, and this would need to be adjusted to find the cash flows required. The net profit before depreciation value is a good approximation of a year's cash flows, and if only income or profit figures are available then adjustments should be made to find this value.

With discounted cash flow techniques such as NPV and IRR, interest payments should be ignored when creating the cash flows for a period. The use of a discount factor already accounts for the costs of finance, and to also include the interest charge costs would see them counted twice and give misleading cash flows and would result in incorrect information being used to make investment decisions.

Finally, investment appraisal methods are simply a tool to support decision-making, and the decision-making process shouldn't be based on them alone. Other factors that may be harder to measure will play a part, such as a feeling that one project is more suited to the strengths of a business than the alternatives, or a greater level of trust with the people who will be involved in a certain project. The varying levels of reliability linked to the forecasted cash flows are also a factor, and some cash flows can be predicted with confidence, while others will be little more than educated guesses.

Surveys suggest that businesses are taking a more rounded approach to the investment appraisal process, and increasingly using more than just one of the four main methods to evaluate projects. The discounted cash flow methods, NPV and IRR, have grown in popularity over the years and are now the most favoured of all appraisal techniques, with larger businesses especially being more likely to use the discounting methods, and to use more than one technique to analyze the projects under consideration.

Yet the ARR and payback period also remain popular despite the significant flaws with them noted earlier, and this is especially true with smaller sized businesses, which are far less likely to use the discounted cash flow methods of NPV and IRR. This may be explained by a desire to avoid complexity in investment appraisal, and a natural tendency not to use something that isn't properly understood.

Of the two discounting methods, IRR is often just as popular as NPV despite its flaws, which may be put down to a preference for a percentage and relative based measure, as managers can see this as having more meaning than an absolute value which requires further analysis.

6.2 Risk Management

There is always going to be risk in business, and the chance that expected projections won't come to pass is a major issue affecting decision-making. This is especially true for investment decisions for two reasons; the size of the initial investment is likely to be significant, and if cash flows don't occur as expected then the effects on the firm can be both huge and long-lasting; and an investment project is typically following a lengthy timescale of at least a few years, which gives more time for things to go wrong between the period of the investment decision and the project's end.

Strategies to manage an investment project's risk can be divided into two distinct categories; an assessment of the level of risk; and a reaction to the level of risk. Most of the work comes with the former, and once the level of risk is known then adjustments can usually be made to deal with it.

Sensitivity Analysis

Sensitivity analysis is a popular method to assess a project's risk level, and it involves a detailed examination of the factors influencing a project, to investigate how changes in these inputs affect changes in the cash flow output. The first step involves an investment appraisal with the most trusted method indentified above, NPV, with informed estimates for each variable input factor, such as sales volume, sales price, initial investment, ongoing material and worker costs, the project's length, and the discount rate. If the project passes the investment appraisal with a positive NPV, then each of these individual factors is changed one at a time to determine the sensitivity of this positive result, and to find out the margin of safety or margin or error that is acceptable for each input. For example, when sensitivity analysis is performed for the initial investment all other factors are held constant at their original estimate, while the cost of the initial investment is raised until the amount corresponding to an NPV of zero is found. The difference between this value and the original estimate would represent the margin of safety for this individual input.

The procedure of conducting sensitivity analysis is very simple and it can be performed easily in an Excel spreadsheet, as the cell containing the relevant input has its value gradually increased or decreased, and the investment manager watches another cell set up to give the NPV of the project. When the NPV equals zero the changed input value is recorded in a new cell, and another calculation gives the difference between this critical value and the original estimate of that input to show the acceptable margin of error, the variation allowed in the input while maintaining a positive NPV and profitable project.

However, sensitivity analysis doesn't give a clear accept or reject rule for a project, and it's still down to the manager to decide if the margin of safety for profitability is large enough. Another problem with sensitivity analysis is that it only considers one input at a time, when in reality several of the inputs may differ from the estimates made in the NPV investment appraisal. To overcome this issue requires the alteration of more than one input variable at a time, a technique known as scenario building. This strategy has grown in popularity with firms over time, as businesses become more cautious in their investment decisions in an increasingly uncertain world.

Expected Net Present Value

In certain circumstances it may be possible to assess the level of risk using statistical probabilities. There may be only a limited range of potential values for each of the NPV input variables, and the associated probabilities of occurrence may be known. This data can be used to give an expected net present value (ENPV), which takes the probabilities of each potential annual cash flow resulting from the range of input values, and forms a weighted average result.

For example, the sales volume and cash flows for a firm's investment project may be directly influenced by the behaviour of a business competitor. An aggressive response from the rival (option 1) could result in lower sales and cash flows, a defeatist withdrawal (option 2) could give greater sales and cash flows with reduced competition, and no response at all (option 3) would give sales somewhere between the two. A firm considering an investment could work out the cash flows corresponding to each possible response from the competitor, and use their own analysis to assign percentage likelihood probabilities to each action. It will be assumed that annual cash flows are the same each year here to simplify matters, but in the event that cash flows were not equal every year the procedure would simply be repeated for each different year. A firm's analysis could give the following results:

Option 1 = £10,000 cash flow, and a 0.1 probability
Option 2 = £60,000 cash flow, and a 0.5 probability
Option 3 = £30,000 cash flow, and a 0.4 probability

Option 1 (aggressive response by competitor) has an expected cash flow of £1,000 (£10,000 x 0.1), option 2 (defeatist withdrawal by rival) has an expected cash flow of £30,000 (£60,000 x 0.5), while option 3 (no response) sees an expected cash flow of £12,000 (£30,000 x 0.4). Combining these three results gives the expected annual cash flow of £43,000 (£1,000 + £30,000 + £12,000). The present value of this amount would then be found for each year of a project, and if the calculated expected NPV was positive then the project should generate profits and get the firm's approval, but if it was zero or negative then the project should be rejected.

ENPV can be useful as it offers a clear result and a decision rule to apply to an uncertain situation. But the expected result may have no chance of occurrence, as this example shows. £43,000 is the expected annual cash flow here, yet the information found by the firm suggests that only £10,000, £60,000 and £30,000 cash flows are possible. But the biggest problem with the ENPV method is that it hides the inherent risk involved in an investment opportunity. The expected result here is a £43,000 annual cash flow, yet two of the three possible options give far lower cash flows, and their combined probability totals 0.5 (0.1 + 0.4) or 50%. That gives a 50% or one in two chance that the actual annual cash flow will be far lower here, yet a firm is meant to decide a project's profitability based on an ENPV outcome. The possibility for misleading results is significant with ENPV, and it's up to firms to keep this in mind during its use. A firm might want to reject an investment opportunity right away if any of the potential cash flows are too low to offer profits.

Assigning Probabilities

The greatest difficulty in risk assessment is determining all of the possible outcomes and then assigning realistic probabilities to them. The reason that risk assessment is required in the first place is precisely because the investment's outcomes are uncertain, and therefore it may be impossible to determine an accurate probability for a future result.

In order to assign probabilities an investor has to make a choice between using the limited information that is available, or relying instead on their own opinion. Objective probabilities are based upon the data gained from past experience, and an investment manager can look at factors such as the recent trends in consumer demand, the historical lifespan of specific physical assets, or the past results for investment projects similar to their own. But this is always a limited approach as the past isn't necessarily a good indicator of the future, and these objective probabilities may have to be modified to account for downturns in market demand, or changes in the design and technology of investment assets. However, at the very least objective probabilities can give a rough estimate of the likelihood of an outcome.

Subjective probabilities come into play when objective probabilities are unreliable or unavailable, and these are based around opinions. These may come from the business managers considering the investments, or alternatively a firm may seek out external experts in the field. But opinions are just that, and they can be biased and flawed, although a unanimous opinion by a range of different voices could make subjective probabilities more reliable.

Adjusting For Risk

Once risk assessment is complete and a project is found to hold an increased level of risk, with the investment's cash flows uncertain, the standard response is to expect and demand a higher return. As explained earlier, this greater return based on the inherent risk of a project is known as the risk premium, with ever greater levels of risk linked with higher risk premium returns. This is expected because the investor could usually find a low level of return with a less risky project, such as risk-free returns with banks savings interest or government bonds, and there would be no reason to select the project with the increased risk unless it offered a greater return.

When faced with increased risk in an investment project a business would normally increase the discount rate used during NPV analysis. This automatically demands a risk premium for the project, as without it the project will have a lower NPV than other less risky competing opportunities and won't be chosen. The lowest possible level for the discount rate would be the risk-free rate, such as the rate of return from protected government stock, which is covered against all of the risk that a business can't avoid. A risk premium would be added to this rate of return to determine the discount rate to use for the riskier project.

A risk-adjusted discount rate may make it easier for managers to assess investment opportunities, and they can approve or reject projects based on NPV values as before. But the difficulty in properly assessing risk remains, and if the assessment on risk levels were incorrect then the risk premiums and risk-adjusted discounting will only compound the error, and poor decisions may be made on investments.

6.3 Project Management

Evaluating already identified projects to select the investment opportunity offering the greatest net cash flows and profit has been the focus of this book, but this is only one step of many in the investment process. Project management can be divided into five separate stages, which must all be performed properly if investment appraisal is to be successful.

1. Decide Resources Available For Investment

The money free for investment may depend upon the amounts that can be borrowed from external sources, or the resources that can be freed internally as a result of changes by management. Either way, the financial resources available may not to be enough to fund all of the most lucrative and profitable investment opportunities. As a result some type of capital rationing may need to occur, where a decision is made to hold back available resources to prevent poor investments from being made. If capital is tight enough then lower cost and reduced scale profitable investment opportunities may be the only ones under consideration, using only part of the available money.

2. Find Profit-Making Projects

Finding profitable projects is a central task in the investment process. Any efficient and ambitious business should have a well designed strategy to identify new feasible investment opportunities. Typically this may be performed internally with a research and development department, but for smaller businesses it can be outsourced to external experts at a cost. If a firm doesn't have a good strategy to identify good profitable investments then they'll all be taken up by business rivals, who will gain internal efficiency and greater market penetration to see the non-investing firm left behind, with its position and even survival in the marketplace at risk. The search for investments will usually involve an extensive analysis of the market to predict upcoming trends, and take advantage of the changing environment and technology, but an internal innovation department may also be able to suggest investment in new ideas.

3. Project Assessment

Each proposed investment idea must be properly screened before a firm is prepared to invest significant amounts of resources into it, and this screening will usually involve a series of set questions such as:

What is the goal of the project?

How does the project's goal compare to current business goals?

What level of investment finance is required?

What other non-financial resources are required?

How long will the project last?

What cash flows are expected?

What is the NPV of the project?

What are the biggest obstacles to the project's success, and how can they be managed?

How much unavoidable risk is associated with the investment opportunity?

Beyond the details of the proposed project itself, there are also issues regarding those responsible for putting it forward for selection and managing it to completion. Even if a project appears to be potentially lucrative, if management lacks faith in those who would be overseeing it then the project may still receive a poor assessment.

4. Project Approval

Once the business manager makes a positive assessment of an investment opportunity and those who would oversee it, then the project can be formally approved. If they're not fully satisfied with the project they may request more information, or instead make some suggestions for alterations, and then come back to reassess the additional information or revised project at a later date. The proposed project may be rejected outright if it appears unprofitable or too challenging, but the consequences and costs of passing on the project should also be fully investigated.

5. Observe and Direct Project

A decision to invest should be followed by the investment actually being made, and managers managing the project through to completion. This process will involve regular observation of the project's status, with frequent communication with the business to report how actual cash flows compare to those forecast before the investment was approved. Any significant deviations from expectations need to be understood and dealt with where possible, and if the completion date or overall cash flows become irredeemably worse this should be reported back to the business, where a decision may be made to change the project's management, or even abandon the opportunity completely in extreme circumstances.

Once the project is over a post-completion audit may be conducted to evaluate if the project met expectations, and where possible improvements could have been made. The results of this analysis will reveal lessons to be learned for the selection and management of future investment opportunities, and highlight the strengths and weaknesses of the firm. Another benefit of conducting a post-completion audit is that it holds those who proposed the project to account, and this should discourage them from making unrealistic and optimistic cash flow forecasts before the project assessment stage, solely to secure project approval and gain firm resources to use as they wish.